T0209344

VICTORIOUS VERSES

VIVIAN ANN TATE

WESTBOW
PRESS®
A DIVISION OF THOMAS NELSON
& ZONDERVAN

WestBow Press books may be ordered through booksellers or by contacting:

WestBow Press
A Division of Thomas Nelson & Zondervan
1663 Liberty Drive
Bloomington, IN 47403
www.westbowpress.com
1 (866) 928-1240

ISBN: 978-1-9736-4264-0 (sc)
ISBN: 978-1-9736-4263-3 (e)

Library of Congress Control Number: 2018912120

Print information available on the last page.

WestBow Press rev. date: 10/23/2018

This book is dedicated to my younger brother Harry R. Tate, currently residing in heaven with the Lord. Harry also expressed his passion for God's Word through Christian prose and poetry.

Acknowledgments

I give thanks to God for directing my path and blessing me with the ability to express my love for Him in this genre. He has given me the words, perspectives, rhymes and connotations for each of these verses... to God be the glory!

I thank my sister Carolyn Eggleston, who served as my primary critic and had to listen to many of these poems before they were finalized.

Last, but most definitely not least, I give special thanks to the awesome women in the Women's II Sunday School Class at Calvary Baptist Church, who blessed me with their continuous encouragement!

Contents

Conquering Fear

2 Timothy 1:7 (KJV)

[7] For God hath not given us the spirit of fear; but of power, and of love, and of a sound mind.

If Only You Can

If you can turn your
Fears into faith
And your tears into trust....

He'll turn your
Pain into praise
And your hurts into hallelujahs!

Down in the Valley

When you're down in the valley of the shadow of death
    where there's no place to go but up,
let go of your fears and cling to your faith,
    as you sip from life's bitter cup.

There's joy in the valley of despair and distress,
    there's growth in each step that you take.
Don't surrender to sorrow, don't dwell in defeat.
    Rebuke all your hurts and heartache.

There's help and healing and hope and happiness
    in the valley where shadows abide.
Let God take control, let Him lead the way,
    let go and let Him be your guide.

Keep your hand is His and your head held up high.
    Let the "Son" light the path for your feet.
He'll show you the way that He wants you to go,
    and protect you from enemies you'll meet.

Joy is a jewel that's grown in the valley
    where shadows and darkness reside.
Just bask in His love and draw on His strength.
    Remember…it's for you that He died.

Let It Shine

Don't tell me who you think I should serve,
　　or what you think I should do.
Don't tell me who you think I should be.
　　I don't need to hear that from you.

You try to tell me how I should act
　　like, "don't publicly bless your food".
I'm thanking God who gave me the food,
　　and I think that you are just rude!

I don't want my fear to shut me up,
　　or scare me into submission.
I need the courage to share my faith
　　and fulfill God's Great Commission.

Pray to God for the courage to stand,
　　knowing someone out there won't approve.
Don't trust yourself, but do trust your God.
　　Ask the Holy Spirit to move.

So, let your courage shine like a star,
　　on a background of velvet black.
Give God praise and give Him glory,
　　because God has got your back!

How to Have Victory in Jesus

The victory we have in Jesus
  is something that we should all share.
So, when you know someone's hurting,
  let them know that Jesus does care.

Tell them about when you suffered
  and how Jesus helped you get through.
And should you learn they don't know Him,
  the introduction is left up to you.

Jesus will give you opportunities
  to share things that He's done for you.
Don't be afraid to be His witness,
  that's not what He wants us to do!

He wants us to be a testimony
  of the many things that He's done for us.
So, don't be afraid to share Jesus,
  don't hesitate or put up a fuss.

Don't forget about His great Commission
  that He expects all of us to do.
He wants us to tell about His goodness
  so that others can experience it too.

Know that God's is not a Spirit of fear,
    but of power, and love, and a sound mind.
So, let the Holy Spirit help you
    leave fear and insecurity behind.

Then you can be a witness for Jesus
    and grow in your relationship with Him.
Your sharing His victory with others,
    will change the lives of many of them.

Defeating Sin

1 Corinthians 15:57 (KJV)

57 But thanks be to God, which giveth us the victory through our Lord Jesus Christ.

The Devil is a Liar

Yeah, the devil is a liar...he's just like most men.
    So few can be trusted...only one in every ten!

Most men?

Where did you get your statistics on sin?
    Some people are liars, both women and men.
The devil could be a woman and may not be a man.
    To entice you to commit sin...he'll be everything he can!

He knows what you want, and he knows what you dream.
    He knows how to lure you, all peaches and cream.
Don't think that he's ugly with horns and a tail.
    He'll use what attracts you to ensure he won't fail.

So, don't look for the devil in the form of a man.
    To convince you to sin, he'll take any form he can!
Don't yield to temptation, turn your back on all sin.
    Know the devil is a liar...whatever form he's in!

Restoration

Is your glass of life half full,
    or do you believe, half empty?
How often we do grumble,
    when we've been blessed with plenty.

Do you try to drown your sorrows
    in possessions, booze or food?
These distractions aren't the answer,
    they just briefly change your mood.

It's easy to lose your focus
    when troubles come your way.
But trust that God is faithful,
    and we just need to pray.

The devil wants to trick you
    and take away all your joy.
He wants your disobedience
    and seeks just to destroy.

Remember, God is faithful
    and wants what's best for you.
He wants you to obey Him
    in the things you say and do.

Distractions won't restore you,
    and they cannot make you whole.
Only Jehovah Rapha
    can restore mind, body, and soul.

Help with Humility

A child of God should be humble,
    not arrogant and puffed up with pride.
Though we may try to deny it,
    we all have pride deep inside.

So, please don't think that it's easy
    living one's life with humility.
No bragging and no more boasting
    may be beyond our ability.

But there is someone who can help you.
    On Him you can call with no shame.
He'll help you to live in His favor,
    if you will just call on His name.

It's a name above all other names.
    It's the name of Jesus, of course!
The help you seek isn't inside you,
    it's in Jesus...let Him be your source.

Lose It...Lose It

Sometimes the road gets rough,
    and sometimes we do get weary.
Our smiles turn into frowns,
    and our eyes get red and teary.

Don't let the devil scare you.
    Don't let him get you down!
Don't give in to temptations....
    don't gain another pound!

God has a special blessing
    He's preparing you to receive.
The devil doesn't like it,
    so tell him to split, back off.... just leave!

Your body is God's temple,
    not St. Patrick's Cathedral.... okay!
Ask God to give you more strength,
    and you'll be victorious each day.

Freedom

John 8:31-32 (KJV)

[31] Then Jesus said to those Jews which believed on Him, "If ye continue in my word, then are ye my disciples indeed;[32] And ye shall know the truth, and the truth shall make you free."

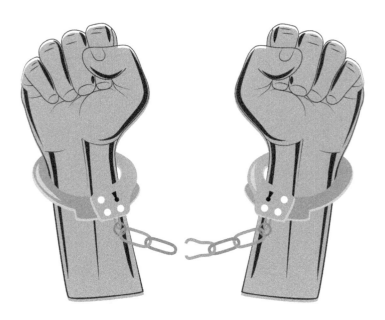

Freedom from Sin

No one on earth is perfect.
    Of this I'm very sure.
We were all born into sin.
    Not one of us is pure.

There is hope. We can be freed,
    from the sin that has us bound.
Jesus died upon the cross,
    and salvation in Him is found.

Invite Him to live in your heart.
    Your belief in Him, express.
Then with a contrite spirit,
    your sins, to Him confess.

He'll come in and change your life.
    Nothing will be the same.
You'll feel like a brand-new creature,
    and Christian will be your new name.

The Road to Freedom

The road to freedom was twisted and rough,
    its travelers were weary and worn.
They walked over hills and through valleys of pain,
    in darkness new suffering was born.

They came here from Africa, in chains, on ships
    to plantations and fields full of cotton.
Their tears and pain, the blood that they shed
    these things should not be forgotten.

Their bodies were broken, their children were sold
    but their voices just could not be stilled.
Their songs, like drums, spoke of faith and of hope,
    spoke of heaven and dreams unfulfilled.

Some could not wait for their freedom to come
    could not live as slaves one more day.
Took all that they had and left in the night
    let Miss Tubman show them the way.

But even though free, the road was still tough,
    life was hard and harsh as a scream.
Segregated and shamed, pushed down and pushed back,
    'til Martin told the world of his dream.

Though the way has been paved, the path is still rough
    and you'll still find some rocks in the road.
Just know what the slaves and what Martin both knew
    that God can help lighten your load.

Who Smokes?

I know I said I would stop, and I will. I just need this one last pack.
  After I smoke all of these I'll quit, and I'll never, ever start back!

Yeah, I did say that seven months ago, and I haven't stopped smoking yet.
  But, I've been through some terrible times, and find relief in my cigarette.

I no longer drink hard liquor, I'm celibate, and try not to lie.
  I don't curse, hurt, cheat or steal…and I don't smoke dope to get high!

All I do is smoke cigarettes…because they really help me with stress.
  Well yes, I really do enjoy it…okay, I like it! I confess!

I know there are so many reasons, why I should break this habit today.
  It's unhealthy, and it can harm others…and just think of the money I pay!

I don't know why I feel so guilty. I mean I'm not committing a sin.
  But the Word calls my body God's temple, and His Spirit does dwell within.

Well, knowing that will stop me, because God's temple should not be defiled.
  If I don't stop, He'll destroy me…but If I do stop, I'm reconciled.

Jesus Christ is my role model, and I must do what He wants me to do.
  Since I can't picture Him smoking…It's not right for "you know who".

That's it! I quit! No more cigarettes to calm me when I get stressed!
I can do this! I know God will help me…and I know that I'll be
blessed!

No more coughing, bad breath or burning holes in my stuff.
Don't smell like a big cigarette, and exercise isn't tough.

My voice is very clear, and now I'm no longer hoarse,
now I really want to sing, but for Jesus, of course.

He did it for me and He'll do it for you, just ask, you'll see, He can't
fail!
Just pray for His help, He can do all things, didn't Jonah escape
from a whale?

Turn it over to Him. Let go and let God. Do it now, right now, don't
delay!
Don't wait 'till tomorrow, come on, stop now! God can free you
today!

God's House

<u>1 Timothy 3:5 (KJV)</u>

[5] *(For if a man know not how to rule his own house, how shall he take care of the church of God?)*

Welcome to God's House

I really do love my church
  but hate that it's started to grow.
So many people have joined
  now only a few do I know.

Some come from other countries.
  I can tell by the way they talk.
And some are just inappropriate
  in how they dress and how they walk.

I really do miss the old days
  when everybody there, I knew.
Now, it just feels different,
  and I just don't know what to do.

God will give me direction
  on whether I go or stay.
And since I need an answer,
  I'll get down on my knees and pray.

Hmph, He told me it wasn't **my** church.
  God said it belonged to Him.
He spoke about obedience,
  said, "Don't judge and don't condemn".

He told me, "Start greeting others,
    and do it with kindness and love.
Help them feel welcome in **my** house.
    and do it with strength from above.

Now, when I go to God's House,
    my actions are not self-defeating.
I've learned how to love my neighbor,
    and everyone gets my greeting!

United We Stand

We say we follow Jesus
    and we claim we really care.
We say we love each other
    and our burdens we will share.

But what we say won't really count
    if it doesn't match what we do.
We must present a united front
    like we're stuck together with glue.

When all the members of a church
    unite on one accord.
Caring, sharing, praying and praising,
    it's precious to our Lord.

Not only will unity help our church
    to prosper and to grow.
It also sends the devil a message
    that it's time for him to go!

My Preacher

I thank God for your teaching,
    (Wow! You even know my name!)
I praise Him for your preaching,
    now my walk is not the same.

I thank Him that your preaching
    Sunday morn and Wednesday nights,
impacts the way I'm walking...
    turns my wrong ways into rights.

Glad you answered when God called you
    and began to preach His Word.
So glad you preach from the Bible,
    so I can trust the things I've heard.

Don't let the devil disturb you
    or persuade you to despair.
Be strong, my prayers are with you
    because this member really does care.

My Pastor

You were appointed by God to perfect the saints;
    a burdensome, difficult calling.

My prayer each day is that God will protect you,
    prop you up and keep you from falling.

I pray His Word keeps you grounded,
    and His love keeps you surrounded!

God Gives the Gifts

The Pastor preached about Spiritual gifts,
    so I thought I would choose which were mine.
Determined that speaking just might be my gift,
    but I always forgot every line.

The Praise Dance members were always so good,
    and I knew I had moves I could show.
I danced till the leader pulled me aside
    and said, "One of us is going to go!"

I knew that my gifts were supposed to be used
    and the one group I'd missed was the choir.
During rehearsal, I screamed out the song!
    They quietly asked me to retire.

As I looked around to see what was left,
    I saw nowhere that my skills would fit.
So, I found a pew in back of the church,
    felt that all I could do was just sit.

But one of the ushers smiled as she passed,
    and asked why I was looking so sad.
Told her my challenge in picking my gifts.
    When she answered, it made me feel glad!

She said Spiritual gifts come from the Lord,
      and we don't get to choose what we get.
Pray that He'll show you the gifts He gave you.
      I know He's not through with you yet.

God answered my prayer and revealed His will.
      What I do every Sunday takes nerve!
I open the doors while wearing a smile,
      I'm an usher, my gift is to serve!

Who Are You Singing For?

Boy did you hear when Lulamae was singing,
    she made that old broken church bell start ringing.

She did all those shrills and trills, dips and skips.
    Her mouth moved so much, you couldn't see her lips.

Did she see a talent scout out in the crowd?
    Because she kept screaming and singing too loud!

She kept turning that microphone this way and that,
    and making wild faces, like she'd just seen a rat.

I can't even remember the words to her song,
    I just know that her singing went on way too long.

All that bobbing and weaving and trying to scat,
    does she know singing worldly is not where it's at?

Then she held that one note till her eyes got all big
    and her whole head started shaking…and so did her wig!

She was moving nobody, and I saw not one tear,
    and when I looked at the Pastor, I think I saw fear.

I can't help but wonder who she's singing for.
    It must be for self, because it's not for the Lord.

Singing real worldly won't get her very far.
    She's singing for Jesus, not singing in a bar.

You know God is watching when you sing for Him?
    When YOU do it all, you may sink and not swim!

Ask Him to take over and sing it THROUGH you.
    Let Him minister to others...you just be His TOOL!

Dancing for the Lord

I want to dance for the Lord;
    not like the twist or jerk.
I want to dance for the Lord,
    but my feet just won't work.

I watched the preacher's wife,
    lose her hat and cut a rug.
But my imitation,
    just got a stare and a shrug.

There must be some big secret
    you must know to really dance.
Some powerful bit of knowledge
    that will help you step and prance.

I guess I'll have to ask her
    how she moves her feet just so.
I hope that she can tell me
    what I really need to know.

Mrs. First lady can you tell me
    how you dance the way you do?
I've tried to imitate you,
    but my feet seem stuck in glue.

She said she couldn't help me,
    but she knew someone who could.
She said if I don't feel it,
    I won't dance the way I should.

What do I need to feel? She said,
    "The presence of the Lord.
Then your feet will move in praise,
    and they'll be on one accord".

I prayed, and I received Him,
    now there's so much joy in me,
I can't keep my feet from dancing,
    because I've got the victory!

He Picked Me

You've been asked to do the welcome
   and you really are afraid.
You're no good at public speaking
   because you stutter, then you fade.

Why, why did she have to ask me?
   I told her that I could not speak.
But she said, "God told me to pick you,
   so, He must not think that you're weak"!

Well, if God told her to choose me,
   then I know He'll help me prepare.
I really shouldn't refuse Him,
   since I know that He'll be right there.

So, God and I wrote out my speech,
   and I shared it with the crowd.
And when I gave God the glory,
   the applause got really loud!

So, when God asks you to do it,
   whatever He wants you to do,
know that He will equip you.
   Just pray and He'll help you get through!

Flowers in our Father's Garden

Their petals are so pretty,
    all sizes, shapes and hues.
Each has so much to offer.
    Never know which ones He'll choose.

Their roots are planted firmly,
    but not in sinking sands.
When storm winds twist and turn them,
    God shields them with His hands.

He cares for and protects them,
    and provides for all their needs.
He never does forsake them,
    even when they act like weeds.

We're just flowers in God's garden
    His seeds we'll strive to sow.
Just flowers in His garden,
    trusting God to help us grow.

Heaven

John 14:2 (KJV)

² In My Father's house are many mansions: if it were not so, I would have told you. I go to prepare a place for you.

The Residence of the Redeemed

I was blessed by God to build a house,
    a new home, not just for me.
On moving day when we moved in,
    it was me and another three.

The Father, Son and Holy Ghost,
    in spirit with me they dwell.
And I'm so glad because of them,
    I've been saved from a burning hell!

I know one day I will move again
    to a new home like none before.
Where the gates are pearl, and the streets are gold,
    and no one up there is poor.

My eternal home will have no sin.
    Everyone up there will be pure.
And our God Himself will live with us.
    Of this one thing I am sure.

So, I'll see you there when we go home,
    to live with our God above.
We'll worship and sing all day and night,
    surrounded by His love.

Get Ready to Move

The time has come to clean your house,
    because you are just passing through.
Your future holds a heavenly home,
    that God is preparing for you.

We don't know when that day will come.
    So, make sure you are ready to move.
Get rid of all your sinful trash,
    and live the way God will approve.

We have been called out of darkness
    to reflect God's light here on earth.
It's a difficult, burdensome task,
    since we have been sinners from birth.

This is easier said than done,
    while we live in our earthly homes.
Because Satan seeks to destroy us,
    and wherever we go…he roams!

So, arm yourself with the Word of God,
    and learn how to keep your home cleaner.
The struggle is real, but you're not alone,
    you can call on the Great Redeemer!

Joy and More Joy

In the midst of my troubles,
    in my times of despair,
joy comes in knowing
    that God's always there.

But as life's tests and trials
    keep coming my way,
I try to stay focused
    on that bright, joyful day.

When I'll come to the end
    of this earthly life's story,
and go up to Heaven
    to my new home in glory.

There's joy in the comfort
    He provides me down here.
and great joy up in Heaven,
    when His presence is near.

Get Right with Jesus

Where will you go when this life ends?
    Do you know what your fate will be?
I pray you'll go to a heavenly home
    because that's where I know I'll be.

You can too, if you accept Christ.
    He promises this in His Word.
Don't wait, for tomorrow may not come.
    You don't want this prayer deferred.

You must ask Jesus to come in
    to live in your heart right away.
Tomorrow is not promised.
    So, get right with Jesus today!

His Will

Hebrews 13:20-21 (KJV)

[20]*Now the God of peace, that brought again from the dead our Lord Jesus, that great Shepherd of the sheep, through the blood of the everlasting covenant,* [21] *Make you perfect in every good work to do his will, working in you that which is wellpleasing in His sight, through Jesus Christ; to whom be glory for ever and ever. Amen.*

You Choose

I know I'm a Christian,
    of that I am sure.
So, is it my fault when
    some thoughts are impure?

How can you blame me
    for the way that I act?
When I live in a world
    full of things that distract.

Sin and temptation
    are everywhere I look!
On TV, my iPad,
    even inside my book!

But that's how the devil
    wants God's child to think.
He can lead you astray
    before you can blink.

Don't look for excuses
    when you misbehave.
Think on God's mercy
    and the sacrifice He gave.

Get rid of those things
    that are distractions for you,
and focus on things
    that God wants you to do.

Maybe your novel
      should be "kicked to the curb".
Then open your Bible...
      God's Word won't disturb!

Make sure that the choices
      you make in this life
are under God's will
      to diminish the strife.

Remember, God's judgement
      will one day take place.
What do you want to hear
      when you meet face-to-face?

His Will

I'll follow His will.
    I'll go where He leads.
I'll do what He wants.
    I'll do what He needs.

I'll die to myself,
    let His will be done.
He gave me new life.
    He gave His own son.

My whole life has changed
    because of His love.
He sent me true peace
    on the wings of a dove.

He's sovereign and holy.
    He's my all and all.
He knows that I stumble,
    but He won't let me fall.

When my load gets heavy,
    He gives me rest.
When Satan attacks me,
    He allows the test.

I know I'm not worthy
    of the price that He paid.
He gave up His life.
    In a tomb He was laid.

I can't tell it all,
    what He's done for me.
He died for my sins...
    His blood set me free!

The Gift

Santa's making a list
    and he's checking it twice.
To see who's been naughty
    and who's been nice.

But if I've been bad;
    did some sinful deed,
Santa can't give me
    the gift that I need.

Santa is a fable,
    a legend, a man;
and he can't forgive me
    like my God can.

That most precious gift,
    only Jesus can give.
He died for our sins,
    so that we might live.

So, although we all sin,
    and fall short of His will.
Let's try to live right,
    God's Word to fulfill.

And never forget that
    Jesus is the reason,
for forgiveness and mercy
    and love in this season.

This Branch

I'm so very busy.
    There's so much to do.
There's never enough time,
    for me to get through.

My work's never-ending...
    always something new.
There's always one more thing
    I find I must do.

I go earn a living,
    get home and start cleaning;
but when I work for God,
    it gives my life meaning!

I don't want to just wither,
    or be tossed in the fire.
I will labor for God,
    and that's my desire.

I will abide in Him,
    and yield to His will.
This branch will have purpose,
    God's will to fulfill.

Your Will Lord

Must I really forgive everyone
    who has treated me bad?
See, they really, did hurt me,
    and I'm still very mad!

I know in my heart
    what you want me to say.
But you just don't know
    what a price I did pay.

Okay, maybe You do know
    just how much it cost.
I mean…You forgave me,
    so my soul wouldn't be lost.

But I'm made out of flesh Lord,
    and I know I'm weak.
So, if I need to do this,
    then your help I'll seek.

I cannot refuse to,
    because You forgave me;
and when I forgive others,
    your favor I'll see.

So, Lord help me do this
    because Your strength I need!
It's Your will I'll follow
    and it's Your Word I'll heed!

Holy Spirit

[38] Then Peter said unto them, Repent, and be baptized every one of you in the name of Jesus Christ for the remission of sins, and ye shall receive the gift of the Holy Ghost.

In His Presence

I am unworthy to be in His presence...
    yet He makes His presence known to me.

No time to prepare, no time to ponder...
    just an immediate drenching in the essence of God.

A fullness that far exceeds the scope of rational explanation
    ...overcomes me.

Tears of awe and tears of comprehension fall freely
    when He touches me with the wisps of His glory

...and draws me into His presence.

Never Alone

I serve a risen Savior
    who no longer lives down here;
but He left His Holy Spirit.
    One whose presence I hold dear.

The Holy Spirit lives inside me,
    to help me do what's right;
and when the road of life turns dark,
    He guides me to the light.

When Jesus died on Calvary's cross,
    if we had been left alone;
temptation might have won control,
    had our power just been our own.

Jesus is coming back some day.
    He's descending in a cloud.
And when He sees this child of His,
    I want to make Him proud.

So, I've asked the Holy Spirit,
    to always be my guide.
I know I'll never walk alone,
    because He lives inside.

The Great Commission

God has blessed us so many times,
    and we don't even have to ask.
All He wants from us in return
    is one very important task.

To tell someone about His Son,
    is what God would like us to do.
Think of where you might be today,
    if none had shared Jesus with you.

It may be hard for some to do.
    Something that's easier ignored.
So, ask the Holy Spirit for help,
    because nothing's too hard for our Lord.

When Jesus returned to Heaven,
    He left us His Great Commission.
If we ignore and don't obey,
    that would be a dire omission!

As unto Him

So many people I pass holding signs;
    should I stop and give each one a bill?
Is this what Jesus would want me to do?
    Would I then be following His will?

How can I tell who is really in need?
    I saw one guy drive away in his car.
And another guy held up a sign that said
    "Need money to buy drinks in that bar".

But if I don't give, won't that offend God?
    Shouldn't our giving be as unto Him?
I'm really perplexed, don't know what to do.
    Should I donate, or not give to them?

Wow! Just remembered where my help comes from.
    Who I call on in times of despair.
No matter what size my problem may be,
    the Holy Spirit is always right there.

So, Lord let me know when you want me to give.
    Tell me who, what, when, where and how.
And help me learn how to give of myself,
    because I'm ready to do that right now!

Your Standard is Higher

We know that we may encounter
    those who modify Your Word.
So please help us with discernment
    to know when false doctrine is heard.

Please bring it to our attention
    when traditions hide your commands.
And help us make corrections
    to avoid your reprimands.

Sometimes we let our traditions
    erode our focus on You.
We quickly see this in others,
    but seldom in those things we do.

So please help with our hypocrisy
    and expose those things that we hide.
Through the power of Your Spirit
    which does in our hearts reside.

Help us to stay steeped in Your Word
    and remember Your standard is higher.
and know that through our obedience
    we will fulfill our Lord's desire.

Leading

Psalms 25:5 (KJV)

⁵ Lead me in thy truth and teach me: for thou art the God of my salvation; on thee I do wait all the day.

Good Luck

It truly does bother me when some people say,
    "You really do have good luck!"

It's Jesus who holds me, helps and protects me,
    and pulls me up out of the muck.

Lady Luck isn't my sidekick like some people think.
    There's another who walks by my side.

He leads me and blesses me, shows me the way.
    It's Jesus who serves as my guide.

Learning to Lead

If you want to find a good mentor,
    and you don't know what to do;
start looking for a good leader,
    someone you can look up to.

Find one who leads by example;
    who is committed to the Lord.
Someone like you who serves Jesus,
    so you can be on one accord.

But please remember this one thing,
    that God has a plan for your life.
Make sure He gives confirmation,
    to prevent bad choices and strife.

Learn all you can from your mentor.
    Hear everything they have to say.
Then one day you'll lead by example,
    helping others to grow in God's way.

How to Say Thank You

The devil has really been busy,
    his attacks just don't seem to stop.
He wants us to stop trusting God,
    because he wants to come out on top.

We need to learn how to ignore him,
    since God has prepared us to stand.
The devil can get nothing from us
    if we just hold on to God's hand.

The Lord will always be there for us
    when we follow wherever He leads
The blessings He bestows are many.
    He'll provide for all of our needs.

So, what can we do to say thank you
    to the God who created it all?
Just worship, and trust and obey Him
    and try to make sure you don't fall.

Humble Yourself

You're not all that and a bag of chips!
　　Don't forget who's brought you this far.
It's God who's given you everything,
　　your talents, your home and your car.

You boast, you brag, it's all about you!
　　Please listen to this strong warning.
Change from your ways or I know you'll feel,
　　the judgement of God one morning.

Humble yourself in all that you do.
　　Remember that God is greater!
Honor His Word, get rid of your pride.
　　Do it now, rather than later!

Live in a way that's pleasing to God.
　　You don't want to kindle His wrath!
Just so you know, you're not in control.
　　It's our God who controls your path.

Prayer

Philippians 4:6 (KJV)

6 Be careful for nothing; but in every thing by prayer and supplication with thanksgiving let your requests be made known unto God.

How We Need to Pray

Every morning, every night,
    every minute, every hour;
praying without ceasing,
    gives you access to God's power.

Pray during the good times,
    and pray when things are bad.
Pray with perseverance.
    When God answers, you'll be glad!

Pray in supplication,
    and petition God for others.
Pray in intercession,
    for you sisters and your brothers.

Don't forget the preacher,
    who teaches God's Word to you.
Pray for his strength and anointing,
    to do what God wants him to do.

When you don't know what to pray for,
    or which words you need to say,
just invite the Holy Spirit in…
    He'll show you how to pray.

Order Your Prayers

They asked me if I would pray out loud,
    which is something that I've never done.
I quickly declared, "I'll pray next week",
    and exited that room at a run.

When I got home, I googled the source
    where I go to get information.
And the thing I learned from their response,
    I'm sharing in this conversation.

The Bible, they said, is just what you need.
    The Lord's Prayer is how you should pray.
Worship, petition, and confess your sins;
    in that order you choose what to say.

I should have gone and asked the true source,
    where all knowledge and wisdom reside.
I should have asked my God for His help
    and let the Word of God be my guide.

I prayed that next week, trusting in God,
    ...not concerned about what they would hear.
Now I'm not only praying out loud,
    but I pray with conviction, not fear.

So, read your Bible, and follow God's will.
    Turn to Him when you're out on a limb.
Order your prayers the way that God wants,
    and you'll find you'll grow closer to Him.

Out of the Darkness

Didn't know who I was, didn't know where I'd been.
  Heard I might not get through one more night.
Doctor said, "She won't talk and may never walk".
  But my church said...oh no that's not right!

Their prayers were with me that very first day.
  They asked for our God to step in.
Prayed me out of the darkness and back into light.
  With Him on my side...I did win!

The power of prayer cannot be denied,
  and my whole life has been rearranged.
I've got a new walk and I've learned how to talk...
  through God all things can be changed!

Temptation

The devil will try to tempt you
   with things that can please your flesh.
But don't give in to temptation,
   Satan's will, and God's will don't mesh.

When Satan tries to tempt you,
   please know you don't have to yield.
For God has given us weapons
   to be used on that battlefield.

See, God knows about temptation
   since Satan did try to tempt Him.
And had Jesus not resisted,
   our futures would be mighty grim.

So, although the devil stays busy
   attacking God's children each day,
remember that your God is greater!
   Just memorize His Word and pray.

Relationships

Hebrews 10:24 (KJV)

24 And let us consider one another to provoke unto love and to good works:

How to Treat Others

As a child of God, I try to do right
    because God sees everything I do.
But, I'm not perfect, and sometimes I slip,
    and I bet the same happens to you.

See, God alone doesn't watch what we do,
    other people may witness our sin.
And when they see us do something wrong,
    our testimony is damaged, right then!

Work hard to please God and follow His will.
    Honor Him in how you act each day.
When you don't know what His will might be,
    just ask...all you have to do is pray.

Be kind to others and treat people right.
    don't discourage, depress or demean.
Remember God and others are watching
    and the example you set will be seen.

Treat others like you want to be treated
    is what the "Golden Rule" tells us to do.
But, here's a rule that works even better,
    treat others the way Jesus treats you!

Precious Relationship

The battles we fight take place each day,
    with the devil, the world and our flesh.
Because the devil is a liar,
    his words and the truth just don't mesh.

The devil wants us to doubt God.
    and to destroy our Christian walks!
So be on your guard and rebuke him;
    and don't listen to him when he talks!

He will succeed if we aren't on guard.
    So, be sure to watch out for his tricks!
He wants you to break God's Commandments,
    when you sin, that's how he gets his kicks!

God does not like disobedience…
    it's a choice to rebel against Him.
One that damages your relationship,
    and your future can turn pretty grim.

So, don't think that God will not punish.
    Even Adam and Eve found that out!
But never forget that He loves you,
    and that should make you want to shout!!

Relationships with God are precious!
    So, work to avoid doing wrong.
When you sin, ask God to forgive you.
    Help your relationship with Him grow strong.

Great Friends

Sometimes you may feel lonely,
    because no one calls on your phone.
You may think you have no friends,
    but you really aren't alone.

Since you have invited Jesus
    to come live inside your heart,
He's your constant companion, and
    from you He'll never depart.

He'll always walk beside you
    and He'll always be your friend.
He loves you and forgives you
    and on Him you can depend.

Really, you have three great friends,
    Father, Son, and Holy Ghost.
They'll never leave or forsake you.
    They'll be there when you need them most.

Just Humble Yourself

Whether family or spouse,
    or even a friend,
most relationships
    have conflicts within.

Big things or little things
    can cause us to fight;
convinced that they're wrong
    ...since we know we're right.

We put up walls when
    things don't go our way.
Or plan our revenge
    to make sure that they pay.

They may let you down
    or really make you mad,
but not making amends
    will just leave you sad.

So, humble yourself,
    it's not just about you.
Ask God for His help.
    He knows what you should do.

And don't waste your time
    thinking life isn't fair.
Just swallow your pride
    and then show that you care!

Friends

If I listen to you when you start to speak,
    then I'll hear what you have to say.
But, if your words aren't enough for me,
    then together we both can pray.

If I'm smart, I'll know I can learn from you
    and your wisdom, I will then seek.
Because I know who you belong to,
    I know through you God may speak.

My hope is that you will level with me
    and tell me what I need to hear.
When I see God's love reflected in you,
    that removes all my distrust and fear.

Having your friendship will liberate me
    from being isolated, depressed and alone.
Because I will know when I need support,
    I can talk to my friend on the phone.

Who Can You Trust

Hoping for honesty
    may be wanting too much,
in a world full of liars
    and cheaters and such.

Not many you can trust in,
    who won't let you down.
It's a wonder we don't greet
    all folks with a frown.

But I know someone
    you can trust like no other;
not your friends, or family,
    or sister, or brother.

I hope you know
    who I'm talking about;
like me you can trust Him,
    of that I've no doubt!

Having faith in God
    can really change your life.
He'll answer your prayers
    and decrease your strife.

God will keep His promises.
    His plan will prevail.
Be thankful our trust rests
    in a God who can't fail.

Soul Mate

Searching here, searching there
    everywhere, every place.
Seeking my true soul mate,
    just looking for his face.

Don't know when I'll meet him.
    I don't know who he is.
I just know that he's praying
    that God will send him his.

I feel that I should know him
    just by the way he talks.
Because he loves my Jesus,
    because in faith he walks.

Sometimes I think I see him
    and my heart will skip a beat.
But if God does not confirm it,
    then I know we'll never meet.

I think that I'll stop looking.
    Yes, I think I'll just let go.
My God knows what's best for me.
    So, I'll let Him run the show.

No more time spent wondering
    just where my soul mate might be
I've turned it over to the Lord
    He knows what's best for me.

Mother

She's eighty today, never been more alive,
    a grandmother to seven, and Mother to five.
A great-grandmother to four, expecting one more,
    truly loves each one and has more love in store.

Climbs three flights of stairs, in the blink of an eye,
    doesn't even breathe hard, while I'm trying to die.
Still has all her teeth, her mind's sharp as a tack,
    She's in excellent health, just has a bad back.

She takes pride in her looks (some men like them too,)
    she still dresses sharp, and her car is brand new!
She takes care of herself, it shows in her smile,
    it shows in her shape, and it shows in her style.

She trusts in the Lord, with a faith that is strong.
    and she won't bite her tongue, if she thinks you are wrong.
Still works in her church, keeps her house spotless too,
    and knows birthdays and all days, that matter to you.

If you ever sit at her table, you will not deny,
    she cooks like an angel, and that is no lie!
She can make tough chicken tender, and really bake a pie,
    but don't eat up all her rolls, or her grandson will cry.

There's no one like Mother, no sir there's not one!
    She's tough and she's tender, she's smart and she's fun.
She's there when you need her, you know that she cares.
    She knows when you're troubled, your worries she shares.

We thank God He blessed her with eighty good years,
    and pray the rest will be better, with no grief, pain or tears.
We thank God He blessed us with a Mother like you.
    We love you, we thank you, and we appreciate you too!

God's Way

Different shapes and colors
    and heights are we,
all of my brothers
    and sisters and me.

The one thing in common,
    is our last name.
Mother and father
    for us were the same.

But often in us,
    a likeness some see,
and I sometimes wonder,
    just how can that be.

It's not how we look,
    but it is how we act.
Same gestures and expressions,
    and that is a fact.

So, if we're God's children,
    can people see this?
Is there a resemblance
    that others can't miss?

Do we act like He does,
    and follow His will?
And love one another,
    His Word to fulfill?

Because God is love,
    He loves everyone.
Loved us so much
    He sacrificed His son.

So, let's love each other,
    and do it God's way,
Let our love be discernible
    ...starting today!

The Right Choice

The road of life has many paths,
    so which one will you choose?
You could go right, you could go wrong,
    but be careful or you might lose.

Choose the straight and narrow highway,
    we know where that one ends.
A life with Jesus as your guide;
    true Christians as your friends.

But if you can't tell friend from foe,
    check out the fruit they bear.
If God is serving as their guide,
    their works will prove them there.

So, build your life on the solid rock.
    Be faithful and obey.
When storms arise, He'll see you through,
    and you'll see His face one day!

Salvation

John 3:16 (KJV)

¹⁶ *For God so loved the world, that he gave his only begotten Son, that whosoever believeth in Him should not perish, but have everlasting life.*

Born to Die

There was nothing she did to earn God's favor.
    In spite of her fears, her faith did not waiver.

Her son was unlike that of any known Mother.
    This child of a virgin resembled none other.

Circumstances of His birth could not have been stranger.
    He was God in the flesh and was born in a manger.

Sent down here to earth just to save you and me,
    in Him our invisible God, man could see.

He's been where you're going and felt what you feel.
    Through His grace and mercy, your pains He can heal.

I pray you meet Jesus and make Him your own.
    Now that I know Him, I'm never alone.

He was born just to die, new life He does bring;
    this man that we worship, our Lord and our King.

The Shepherd

People search for joy, in all the wrong places,
    and look for love, from all the wrong faces.
People drink, and smoke, and wander around;
    dance and party, and in sin can be found.

They're lost right now and have fallen off track.
    They need someone who can guide them all back.
Like the Shepherd who herds His sheep each day,
    and finds all the lost ones who've gone astray.

He'll show them true peace, and joy, and love.
    They'll know He's present, inside and above.
This Shepherd they'll find is also a friend,
    whose forgiveness and caring, will never end.

They'll learn of His goodness, mercy and grace;
    of His constant help, when in a dark place.
If they call on His name, and confess their sin,
    He'll be their guide, and new life will begin.

He'll be their Shepherd, for them He'll provide.
    He'll never leave them, in them He'll abide.
They'll no longer be lost, because now they're found.
    They won't go to hell. They're now heaven bound.

Right Now

Been searching and searching, don't know what I'm looking for,
    but I know I'll be fulfilled, if I open the right door.
So many doors I've opened, so many places I've been,
    so many things I've done, and some of it was sin.

I thought I'd done enough good to outweigh all the bad.
    I thought I'd go to Heaven…and that's what's really sad.
Oh yes, I went to church…at least two times every year.
    I thought I was paying attention but didn't really hear.

Finally, heard the story the preacher was trying to tell…
    Jesus died on Calvary's cross to keep me out of hell.

When they said, "Come to Jesus", I thought, "no, not today.
    First, I'll get my act together, then see if Jesus is the way."
They said, "Come as you are, He'll wash you white as snow."
    I thought life would then be boring, so I just said, "No."

I told them my life was sinful and I needed to clean up a bit.
    They said, "A fish cannot be cleaned before the fisherman
    catches it!"
Told me that Jesus would accept me, just the way I was,
    and then He'd wash away my sins, since that's what Jesus does!

My whole life would be changed, and I'd be a brand new creature.
    I'd know fulfillment, joy and peace, with Jesus as my teacher.
They said, "Accept the Lord today…He'll supply your every need.
    Life can be rich and rewarding, if you just let Jesus lead."

I invited Jesus into my heart; just knew I shouldn't wait another day,
   for tomorrow is not promised…and hell is the penalty for delay!
So those of you who are waiting, please take this word of advice.
   It's too costly to postpone salvation, believe me you won't like
   the price.

Seeking Perfection

Even though you've been saved
    and have obviously thrived;
until you meet Jesus,
    you have not arrived!

Salvation took a moment
    but perfection takes time.
Being lazy in Jesus,
    just might be a crime.

Open up your Bible and
    stop twiddling your thumbs.
You'll need to be ready
    when that day finally comes.

Observe those around you
    who's lives reflect God's Son.
Follow in their footsteps,
    to find out how it's done.

Then, join an assembly;
    listen to someone preach.
Just make sure that their walk
    matches everything they teach.

Then, on that bright morning
    when you depart from this place.
You can hold your head high
    when you look into God's face.

In His Light

We live in a world full of darkness.
    Where people make wrongs into rights.
Where evil and hatred are common.
    Would someone please turn on the lights!

Thank God, for He sent us a Savior.
    His Son came to show us the way.
He'll show us the path to salvation,
    and help turn our dark nights to day.

He promised that if we would follow,
    then we'd have the "Light of Life".
He'll never leave nor forsake us,
    He'll help during troubles and strife.

In your life make God the center.
    Put everything else all around.
Trust Jesus to teach you and guide you,
    in His light true peace can be found.

Watch Your Step

I've never walked in your shoes,
 suffered your blues, or
  paid any of your dues.

Never felt all your pains,
 your storms or your rains,
  your losses or gains.

Don't have to go where you've been
 or experienced your sin,
  to know how to win.

When it's Jesus you choose,
 I know you can't lose
  and that is good news!

So, don't wait another day,
 let Him lead the way
  what more can I say.

Let your heart be your guide
 and swallow your pride,
  ask Him in to reside.

That's all you have to do
 to feel like brand new,
  and you'll walk better too!

How Do We Compare

We compare ourselves to others,
  what we own, even what we earn.
Do we care that they are better?
  Should that really be our concern?

The Joneses live next door to you
  and they watch your every move.
They think that you compete with them
  but you have nothing to prove.

Don't start trying to live like them.
  Or willingly play their game.
Instead, devote all of your time
  glorifying our God's name.

The Bible says, "none are righteous",
  we all are sinners, everyone.
And that means no one is better,
  so, compare yourself with none.

The standard that we should desire
  is one we will never achieve.
If we compare ourselves to Jesus,
  our sins we will truly perceive.

Nobody on earth is perfect,
  we're all sinners, you and me.
But we can be forgiven,
  since Jesus died to make us free.

Seniors

¹⁴ They shall still bring forth fruit in old age; they shall be fat and flourishing;

Seasoned Saints

We've been here long enough to know....
 what's right from what's wrong, what's weak from what's strong,
  praises from complaints...we are seasoned saints.

Through life's lessons we've learned ....
 that the devil's a liar. Our souls are on fire.
  God is our source...and we're His, of course!

Experience has taught us....
 to let God be our guide, know from Him you can't hide,
  know that talk is just cheap...and your walk is what's deep!

Young people.... should not have to....
 go where we've been, to identify sin,
  know it's not just a game...when you call on His name.

Though you may not know us....
 please hear what we say, learn how to pray.
  Let God direct your path...and **don't** experience His wrath!

He wants you to know that....
 His yoke is easy! Satan's is slick and sleazy!
  and when you try to live right...you'll sleep good at night!

So please hear what we're saying....
 and choose Jesus for your life. He'll help conquer your strife.
  He'll help with all you do...He'll make your life brand new.

Hey, our lives are not yet over....
  though our bodies may sicken, and our clocks are really tickin'.
  Our changes may be drastic...but our futures are fantastic!

When we think about tomorrow....
  we know where we will be.... that we'll finally be free.
  We won't feel pain, and we won't feel old,
    Because we'll be walking on streets made of gold!

Older and Wiser

Her shoes were so cute, that I bought some too;
    spending money on shoes I didn't need.
Sometimes we don't always do what we should
    and our hunger for new things we feed.

It's so hard to save and easy to spend,
    because money burns a hole in your pocket.
You want to be wise in handling your funds,
    But when advice comes your way you just knock it.

But you'll be older and wiser some day
    and that's when you'll think about retiring.
If you don't plan and save for that time,
    you'll be looking for someone who's hiring.

See, sometimes your will and God's aren't the same,
    and things won't turn out like you've planned.
You don't control what your future will hold,
    God does...so hold on to His hand.

You will have good times and bad times too.
    When you need help, pray and just ask it;
and pray that He'll share His wisdom with you,
    then you'll have the strength to get past it.

Seasoned

I am the salt of the earth,
    you can see it in my hair.
You can tell by my walk,
    that I'm in my Father's care.

When trials come, and you need to talk,
    get someone who knows the score.
Just find yourself a seasoned saint
    who's been in that place before.

Though my body grows weak,
    my mind's sharp as a tack.
If you say you don't need Jesus,
    I'll tell you, that's just whack!

Yes, I know what that word means
    I know lots of other words too.
But the words that mean the most,
    are those He sent to you.

Use the Bible as your yardstick,
    and measure everything you do.
Let His Word direct your steps,
    and let Jesus see you through.

Turn away from all that's sin,
    and hold the things of my Lord near.
When I speak these words of wisdom
    don't pretend that you don't hear.

Don't close your mind to Jesus.
Open your heart, ask Him in.
I know He'll lead and guide you,
because you're going where I've been.

Stress

3 And not only so, but we glory in tribulations also: knowing that tribulation worketh patience;

Lord Help Me

Lord help me, please help me. I really am stressing.
  It feels to me like I just need a blessing.
My car needs fixing, and my roof sprang two leaks.
  My bank account's empty, and will be for two weeks.
I've got health problems too, and I'm in constant pain.
  Seems like the less food I eat, the more weight I gain.

Lord help me, please help me, my life is depressing,
  and I think it's because the devil's been messing.
I try to live right, and I try not to sin.
  I stay in the Word, but I still just can't win.
I really am lonely, and need a soul mate,
  But men just ignore me...all I want is a date!

Lord help me, please help me, I need time for resting.
  God is it you who's been doing some testing?
If I walk what I talk, and change to new ways,
  could I expect sunshine to fill some of my days?
My moaning and groaning make my pressure raise.
  Maybe instead I should give God some praise.

I know what I'm feeling, since I know where I've been,
  but God hasn't left me, and I know we will win.
So, I'll open my mouth and shout "to God be the glory"!
  I won't sit here moping, I'll trust Him...not worry!
Lord help me, please help me, I forgot whose I am
  I know nothing can defeat me...I belong to the Lamb!

Who's Comforting You?

This week has been so difficult
    that I'm feeling really stressed.
I'm anxious and I'm all tensed up
    and in every way distressed!

I feel I need some comforting,
    and think it's in something to eat!
Like ice cream, cake or candy,
    just to give myself a treat.

Why do I always reach for food?
    Is this just some kind of test?
Is the devil trying to tempt me?
    Should I give the food a rest?

Since it's comfort that I'm seeking,
    gaining weight would make me sad.
I need something else to calm me…
    something that will make me glad.

My consolation isn't in food,
    or money, or things possessed.
It's in the one who died for me,
    for He can calm me best!

Through me He can calm others,
    with testimonies that I share.
To let them know how God helped me,
    remind them He's always there.

Don't forget who you should turn to
    when life's trials have you stressed.
Remember God is always there,
    turn to Him and you will be blessed.

What Job?

My boss just called me in...told me of a reduction in force.
Told me I had four whole weeks...and he'd be a reference, of course.

Told me I really shouldn't worry.... I'd find a job real quick.
Said it'll all work out just fine...felt like I would be sick.

What about my bills? What about my rent? What about that car I just bought?
Why another trial? Why another test? Why after all the battles I've fought?

I just knew that I would work here...for many, many more years.
But, no promotions left for me, just crushed dreams, fears and tears.

I don't know what to do and don't know where to turn.
My head is hurting; my stomach's starting to churn.

Well, I sure know I can't fix it. I can't do a single thing!
I'll just give this one to my Father...and my Father is a King.

Sometimes when I go through fierce storms, I forget I'm not alone.
I only need to call Him....and I don't even need a phone.

I know He'll see me through....and He'll provide my every need.
I just need to let it go and allow my Father to lead.

When I worry, I'm not trusting Him....and doubt things will work
out okay.

He's never left me, forsaken or failed me, so why do I worry
that way?

I should trust in Him with all my heart, and lean not to my own
understanding.

I should follow where the Lord leads me, and let Him do all the
commanding.

Well, I've turned this over to my Father, and He's removed my anger
and wrath.

In all my ways I'll acknowledge Him, and He **will** direct my
path.

The Bible

Psalm 119:105 (KJV)

[105] *Thy word is a lamp unto my feet, and a light unto my path.*

Deep Down in Your Heart

Even though your spirit is willing,
    your flesh will reveal that it's weak.
The devil will use this against you,
    it's your failure and death he does seek.

But thank God He left us His roadmap
    that helps us stay on the right path.
You don't want to yield to temptation.
    You don't want to deal with God's wrath.

God's Word is a wonderful treasure.
    So, study, believe, and share it.
The more we read, the less we will sin.
    Apply it, obey it, don't quit.

So, hide God's Word deep down in your heart.
    Don't let the devil distract you.
Study and learn, grow closer to God.
    Reflect Him in everything you do.

The Bible tells us how we should live.
    It helps us know which way to go.
When you feel lost, just trust in God's Word.
    you don't have to go with the flow.

His Word

We thank God for Jesus.
It's for us that He died.
We thank Him for His Word.
It serves as our guide.

As we travel life's road,
His Word gives direction.
It tells us the answers,
and even gives correction.

We should follow God's Word.
It's our Christian duty.
There's no other book like it.
It's filled with such beauty.

His Word we should treasure,
through it God does speak.
When our problems need answers,
His Word we should seek.

So, let's study God's Word,
learning all of its parts,
and retain what we've learned
...hidden deep in our hearts.

Do What's Right

Do you remember these words of choice,
    from a really, really old song?
They said, "I don't want to be right
    .... if loving you is wrong"!

It's a song about some choices,
    and we all must make a few.
But always strive to choose what's right,
    because God sees all that we do!

The Bible gives us guidance
    when tough choices come our way.
It teaches us what's right from wrong,
    and compromising's not okay.

As each day brings us new choices,
    choose what's pleasing in God's sight.
Ask Him to give you the courage,
    to choose to do what's right!

Fruitful Living

I'm trying to be more fruitful;
    that's how we're supposed to live.
So, should I try to buy more stuff
    and be more competitive?

I wasn't sure what fruitful meant
    until I found it in God's Word.
There are two ways to be fruitful,
    and both you've probably heard.

The first is to be a witness.
    Share Christ with those who don't know.
Winning others to God's kingdom
    is how fruitfulness can grow.

The second is obedience
    by showing God's spiritual fruits.
Your lifestyle should be a mirror
that reflects your Biblical roots.

So, in order to be fruitful,
    obey God, and share His love.
When things are pleasing in His sight,
    He'll send blessings from above.

One Size Fits All.

I wanted to go shopping
    so, I went down to the mall.
Found a really cute sweater
    that said, "one size fits all".

But wow, when I put it on,
    my arms didn't fit the sleeves.
I couldn't even bend them;
    "one size fits all" deceives!

So, then I moved on to the shoes
    and asked them for size nine.
Tried on the shoes they brought me.
    The pain they caused was a sign.

Our standards are not perfect.
    On them we cannot rely.
So, what then can we count on?
    Whose truth is not a lie?

Well, I can answer that question
    and solve this problem for you.
Know you can count on your Bible,
    because the Word of God is true!

Through the good times and the bad times,
    let God's Word become your guide.
Then follow His direction,
    and trust that He will provide.

Know that God's Word is perfect,
and it, you can always trust.
It tells us how we should live
and pleasing God is a must!

You Have the Victory

There's so much evil around us,
    sometimes demons on every side.
Be sure you don't ignore them,
    just know that from them you can't hide.

See, they know who you belong to
    and they know who holds your heart.
Their number one objective is
    to force you and God apart.

Please don't let them convince you
    to turn away from your Lord.
Your weapons are in your Bible.
    God's Word is your two-edged sword.

So, when the demons come for you
    please don't give in to your fear.
With faith, you can defeat them.
    With Christ, your victory is clear!

About the Author

Vivian Ann Tate has spent more than 30 years managing or directing Diversity and Inclusion in six different Fortune 500 companies. The challenges and struggles associated with her field of expertise, former married life, single parenting, and attempts to earn a graduate degree while working full time, have all been addressed and resolved through her relationship with Christ. Her personal victories, as well as the victorious testimonies of others, are reflected in the poems in this book. Vivian expresses her powerful faith through her poetry with the hope that, as a result, someone who doesn't know Christ may be convinced to accept Him and experience His sustaining love, hope and joy.

Printed in the United States
By Bookmasters